VITAMINS

Teachings of

THE ORDER OF CHRISTIAN MYSTICS

VITAMINS

Teachings of The Order of Christian Mystics

The "Curtiss Books" freely available at

www.orderofchristianmystics.co.za

VITAMINS

THEIR ORIGIN, SOURCES AND SPECIFIC USES

A Supplement to his well known book "Health Hints"

By Dr. Frank Homer Curtiss

The specific effect of each vitamin is fully described in
non-technical language, and the sources from which it can easily
and inexpensively be obtained are listed.

An invaluable aid for all who are suffering from any bodily,
nervous or mental ailment.

2015 EDITION

REPUBLISHED FOR THE ORDER BY
MOUNT LINDEN PUBLISHING
JOHANNESBURG, SOUTH AFRICA
ISBN: 978-1-920483-01-2

"Ministers of Christ and Stewards of the Mysteries of God."

1 Corinthians 4 vs. 1

PART I. GENERAL CONSIDERATIONS

In the first edition of our recent volume, *Health Hints*, we stated that all diseases have acidosis and toxemia as a basic condition, due largely to wrong combinations of food and faulty elimination. Nevertheless, many disorders are specifically due to a deficiency in certain vitamins and mineral salts. While the wide range of diet recommended in our book, especially the use of all the raw and live foods possible, will ordinarily supply all the vitamins and cell-salts needed, nevertheless a general knowledge of the specific effects of the vitamins and the sources from which they can easily be obtained, will help you so to arrange your diet as to obtain the extra amounts needed to supply the evident deficiencies, and thus more quickly overcome their unhappy results. Hence we will give a brief and simplified resume of this complicated subject.

Vitamins are important food substances which are not only essential for the growth, vigor and continued health of the body, and the normal regulation of its glands and other functions, but also for protection of the body from disease. For certain vitamins give specific protection, such as the anti-scurvy, anti-rachitic and anti-infective vitamins etc. Therefore the diet should always contain such protective foods as raw vegetables and fruits, egg-yolks, milk etc. to provide safeguards to the health not found in sufficient quantities in other foods.

Many research authorities now believe that most maladies formerly attributed to toxines, as well as to the improper functioning of the endocrine glands, are primarily due to vitamin and mineral-salt starvation.

The lowered organic functioning thus induced permits the accumulation of toxines and acids and lowers the body's normal resistance to bacterial infections.

While the vitamins are not the materials used in building tissues and producing energy, they do furnish the material from which the endocrine glands produce their specific secretions, upon which all the physiological functions of the body depend. Without them the food is not properly elaborated or assimilated, and hence toxic waste is produced which must be eliminated with a great drain on the vitality.

Vitamins may be considered as the vital essence or soul of the food, as contrasted with the building materials. Since vitamins are formed by the vital life-processes of Nature, artificial or synthetic vitamins are not advocated. For while they may contain the same percentages of chemical constituents they do not contain the "vita" element which is imparted only by the life-currents of Nature. Radionic examination of the wave-length and effects of certain synthetic vitamins shows them to be distinctly depressing to the vitality-index and heart action, and in some cases to be actually poisonous.

Single vitamins can now be obtained at drug and food stores, but some of these concentrations are so powerful that their indiscriminate use may cause grave endocrine unbalance. For instance, excessive use of vitamin D, now so much exploited in the advertisements of irradiated foods, can cause grave kidney disorders. Severe and persisting damage can be done to the lungs, kidneys and large blood vessels by repeated large doses of viosterol. To give concentrated doses of such potent materials without expert advice is nothing less than reckless experimentation. On the other hand, a vitamin A deficiency can induce susceptibility to infection of the heart valves;

deficiency of B can weaken its nervous control and cause muscular weakness, while deficiency in vitamin C can cause shortness of breath, palpitation and rapid respiration. Therefore, unless you can have expert advice, it is far safer to supply the needed vitamins through regulation of the foods naturally containing them in abundance, as listed herein.

The need for different vitamins varies with each individual. Since the vitamins act co-operatively, deficiency diseases are usually due to a lack of several. Therefore it is best to *supply an abundance of all* and let Nature make her own selection.

The hormones elaborated by the endocrine glands are now believed to be formed by the splitting of the vitamin molecule. And it is far more difficult to supply the many hormones formed by the different glands than to supply the few vitamins from which they are made. As one authority says: "Supply the vitamins and Nature will supply the hormones."

So far seven vitamins have been isolated.[1] They are named A, B, C, D, E, F and G. Those soluble in fat are A, D, E and F. They are found chiefly in the protective foods such as vegetables, fruits, milk, fish-oil and nuts rich in fat. Vitamins B, C and G are soluble in water and are found largely in foods rich in water, especially in fruits.

Most meats contain relatively small amounts of vitamins, and those are largely destroyed by the high temperature (350° to 450°) necessary for cooking. In general, steaming is less apt to destroy the vitamins than other forms of cooking, as most of them survive temperatures up to 194°, but the shorter the cooking and the less water used the better. Vitamins D, E and G are not destroyed at ordinary cooking temperatures.

---

[1] Several of these have been split up, and others are being discovered, but these are the fundamental ones and meet the general needs.

Pasteurization of milk destroys vitamin C, while irradiation with ultra-violet light to increase the amount of vitamin D kills vitamin C, so vitamin D is the only one left in pasteurized milk.

As a rule there is less destruction of vitamins in foods cooked at high temperatures for a short time than cooked at low temperatures for a long time. Also the less water used the less vitamins are dissolved out and lost if the water is thrown out. If much water is used it should be saved and used in gravies, sauces or as a vegetable drink. A number of attractive different colored drinks can thus be made from spinach, carrots, beets, peas etc.

Altho most foods contain more than one vitamin, the foods listed herein are chosen because they contain the largest amount of the vitamins under which they are listed. Thus, while nearly all salad greens are especially rich in vitamin A, they also contain fair to good amounts of B, C and G.

Food stuffs that do not contain vitamins may be regarded as dead foods, as they contain no building materials such as mineral salts, proteins, etc. Such foods supply fuel and temporary energy only. They include all white flour and *all the many products made from it.* It is not only de-vitaminized and de-mineralized but it is also bleached. And the bleaching necessary to keep white flour from spoiling leaves certain nitrates in it whose cumulative effects are poisonous. Test animals die from mineral and vitamin starvation in 3 or 4 weeks when fed on white flour products alone, while maintaining their health indefinitely on whole wheat products.

Most manufactured starches, highly refined cereals, polished rice, farina, pearl barley etc., belong to this dead food class. They do not furnish proper food even for insects or germs, hence they can be handled

commercially when stale without loss from "spoiling."
All cereals products and breadstuffs should be made
from the whole grain only. In arterio-sclerosis whole
wheat and brown rice are of decided value, owing to
their large phosphate or phytin content.

The dead foods also include refined or white sugar,
candy, corn syrup and all their products. Their use
temporarily satisfies hunger without supplying the
necessary nutriment for growth. Their use causes the
user to refuse the body-building foods vitally needed.
Children fed on such foods are usually disobedient
and unruly. Instead of being punished, such children
should be put on a diet containing the correct vitamins.
The natural craving for sweets can easily and safely
be satisfied by such live and natural sweets as raisins,
dates, figs, honey, sugar-cane, maple sugar or syrup or
raw, unrefined brown sugar and their products. Raisins
are also said to satisfy the craving for cigarettes and
liquor. Reach for a raisin instead of for a cigarette.

All edible green leaves — lettuce, spinach, turnip
and beet tops, celery etc. — are the only foods that
contain *an excess* of mineral salts and vitamins A and C.
Hence they should be used *daily*, although their mineral
content depends upon the amount of minerals in the soil
in which they are grown, hence varies greatly.

Vegetable juices, obtained by using an extractor or
mine, are more valuable than fruit juices as sources of
both minerals and vitamins, although citrus fruit juice
is a good source of vitamin C. Fresh meats, fowl and
fish are good sources of the growth-promoting vitamins
A and G, but cold storage meats, according to the U.S.
Bureau of Agriculture Bulletins, are valueless for this
purpose.

Warning! While the proper use of vitamins as
described herein will supply the deficiencies indicated,
their use alone cannot be expected to restore one to

perfect health unless the *proper combinations* of foods are observed, and unless acidosis and toxemia are avoided and eliminated. Directions for the many other physical and mental conditions necessary for the maintenance of perfect health are fully described in our *Health Hints*.

PART II. VITAMIN SOURCES AND EFFECTS

Vitamin A. The Anti-infective Vitamin

Vitamin A stimulates growth, but is necessary at all ages. Its deficiency results in loss of appetite, weakness, retarded growth and especially favors lowered resistance to infections or "colds" of the mucous membranes, such as in the eyes, ears, nose, sinuses, glands of the mouth and throat, the gastro-intestinal tract, and sometimes the kidney (nephritis) and bladder (cystitis).

Its deficiency also causes gall-stones and gravel or sand in the kidney and bladder, secondary anemia, psoriasis and favors dropsy from kidney trouble. Such cases, as well as cystitis and albuminuria in the urine without adequate cause in children, are successfully treated by its administration. Although the dissolving of kidney stones is a slow process, the administration of vitamin A promptly allays the irritation. Mottled, ruddy complexion, also "whiskey nose" clear up in a few days by the use of vitamin A.

Its use alone in an infectious attack is not sufficient to check it because vitamin B is also needed to promote toxic elimination, vitamin C to promote white-cell activity, and vitamin D to maintain the blood-calcium balance.

Spinach contains all the vitamins save F. The other salad greens are rich in A, B and C.

Vitamin A helps constipation by its stimulating action on the liver. It is the distributor of potassium to the nervous tissues. Its absence results in sterility.

The earliest symptoms of its deficiency are in the intestinal tract.

It is soluble in fat, but only slightly soluble in water. It is little affected by ordinary boiling or baking, but is destroyed by frying.

It is found in most concentrated amounts in all green leaves commonly used for salads, all green and yellow vegetables, such as broccoli, carrots, yellow or green squash, yellow corn, sweet potatoes, green beans and peas, asparagus, okra, tomatoes, avacadoes, cantaloupes, apricots, bananas, cherries, peaches, prunes, mangoes, olives and dates. Whole raw milk, cream, butter, nearly all fats, cheese, egg-yolks, fish-oils, liver and roe, red salmon and oysters are also important sources of Vitamin A.

Vitamin B. The Anti-neuritic and Heart Vitamin

Vitamin B is necessary for the normal tone of the unstriped muscles of the digestive tract and the blood vessels. Hence its deficiency causes loss of appetite, enlarged, flabby colon, constipation, venous dilation causing vericose veins, hemorrhoids and flabby heart action.

Its absolute lack causes nervous irritibility, and the nerve degeneration of Beriberi.

It is important during pregnancy and improves the quantity and quality of the milk in nursing mothers, and supplies the baby with its needed amount of this vitamin. The albuminuria of pregnancy is due to the deficiency of A and C in the kidneys.

Vitamin B is a natural physiological stimulant and is necessary for the absorption of starches and sweets, and for the nourishment and normal activity of the nervous system. Hence it protects the body from certain nerve and brain diseases.

It is therefore indicated in Beriberi, neuritis, neurasthenia, hyper-thyroidism, toxic goiter, also weak stomach and bowel action by stimulating peristalsis. It is also necessary for the formation of insulin in diabetes.

Owing to its tonic effect on the blood vessels, vitamin B is especially helpful in heart conditions and in preventing and reducing edema. It also prevents nervous and muscular weakness of the heart. Investigators have *caused* and *cured* heart enlargement in test animals by withdrawing and later replacing vitamin B in the diet. It is now believed that the increasing death rate from heart disease is largely due to the increasing use of devitalized foods deficient in vitamins and mineral salts.

Vitamin B is an important factor in treating pernicious anemia and in diabetes where it gradually replaces insulin.

Its deficiency causes pathological enlargement and dysfunction of the whole system of endocrine glands. An excess causes sterility in rats. But hyperthyroid conditions require an excess in humans.

The list of foods containing vitamin B is long, as most vegetables, fruits and meats contain some.

It is more readily destroyed by heat than vitamin A, but little is destroyed if not boiled over an hour; but the less cooking the better.

Since it is readily soluble in water its foods should be cooked in patapar paper so it will not be lost.

It is destroyed by alkalies, hence soda should not be used in cooking.

Nail-biting and thumb-sucking are said to be cured in 10 days by adding liberal amounts of this vitamin and also vitamin D to the diet.

Its best sources are salad greens, carrots, cabbage, asparagus, peas, parsnips, sweet potatoes, fruits, whole grain cereals, (brown rice, oats, barley, rye, wheat), and most nuts.

Other good sources are fish-roe, oysters, egg- yolks, whole milk, buttermilk, meats, liver, kidneys, heart, brains and honey.

Vitamin C. The Anti-scurvy, and Tooth Vitamin

Vitamin C is essential for the growth and health of the teeth and bones. Its deficiency results in bleeding gums, loose teeth, pyorrhoea, sore joints, rheumatism and easily broken bones. Tooth trouble rapidly disappears when a liberal amount of Vitamin C is added to the diet. Supplying vitamin D alone is not enough.

Its deficiency results in loss of appetite and weight, weakness, rapid respiration and heart action, also scurvy.

Owing to its tonic effect on the blood vessels and capillaries, its lack causes dilated blood vessels with capillary hemorrhages, tendency to bruise easily, and black-and-blue spots. On this account its lack is a factor in producing stomach and intestinal ulcers.

Although both vitamins C and B are essential for maintaining the normal tone of the blood vessels, vitamin C is especially valuable in nervous heart conditions of youth and middle age, especially palpitation, shortness of breath, high blood pressure, and also low blood pressure when due to impaired adrenal function.

Its lack is also a factor in thyroid and goiter disorders, anemia in children due to impaired iron absorption, as it is essential to the absorption of oxygen. Anemia which resisted treatment by iron has been cured by lemon juice.

Combined with vitamin E it is effective in vericose veins.

Being essential for the production of mucin which protects the digestive tract from self-digestion, its lack favors stomach and intestinal ulcers, as it allows dilation and congestion of the capillaries.

Together with vitamin B it is essential for the normal function of the thyroid and adrenal glands, being more effectual than iodine.

With B it also promotes the activity of the white blood cells, and co-operates with D in regulating calcium absorption, diffusing it to the tissues from the blood. It is also valuable in tuberculosis.

It is easily destroyed by heat, even at low temperatures, also by alkalies, such as soda etc. With the exception of tomatoes (whose acid preserves it) cooked foods cannot be depended upon for this vitamin, although the skin and outer layers of baked potatoes is a good source of it.

It is not stored up in the body, hence *raw fruits and vegetables* containing it should be eaten *every day*.

Its most valuable sources are citrus fruits, salad greens, cabbage, turnips, cauliflower, asparagus, tomatoes, radishes, rutabagas, berries, canteloups, most raw fruits, sprouted grains, bean sprouts, also raw milk, brains, kidneys and liver.

Vitamin D. The Rickets Vitamin

Vitamin D controls the absorption of mineral salts, especially calcium and phosphorus. Without it the minerals needed for building teeth and bones cannot be absorbed, hence stunted growth and deformed bones (rickets) result.

Even if there are ample amounts of minerals and vitaminic C in the diet, without a good supply of vitamin D they cannot be absorbed, for D is required to enable C to store up the calcium. Without D the calcium phosphate will even be taken from the bones to supply the calcium needed by the blood, thus weakening the bones. Vitamin D enables the blood to both absorb and diffuse the calcium to the tissues.

These alkaline phosphates are found in abundance only in wheat bran. But wheat bran is very irritating to the intestines, hence should not be eaten alone, and only in small quantities. It should always be especially finely ground.

Since both calcium and phosphorous are essential to the nerves, a lack of D results in a marked increase in nervousness, irritability and insomnia. Its lack in children especially results in restlessness, quarrelsomeness, low resistance to infections, and predisposes to pneumonia, tuberculosis and stomach ulcers.

Sunstroke is largely due to a vitamin D toxicosis due to too high a percentage of blood calcium.

Nature expects the animal to get vitamin D largely from the Sun, for the skin contains a small amount of *ergosterol* which is changed into vitamin D by the ultra-violet rays of sunlight, hence the efficiency of sun-baths for rickets. Because of this fact people in very sunny parts of the southwestern states are apt to have many wrinkles and a weather-beaten appearance because of an excess of vitamin D formation in the skin by the excessive sunlight. Persons exposed to excessive sunlight should therefore drink freely of oatmeal water or eat oatmeal because its vitamin F counteracts vitamin D. But an excessive diet of oatmeal may induce rickets because it prevents the absorption of calcium by vitamin D.

Synthetic vitamin D (irradiated ergosterol) is greatly inferior to that found in natural sources, 40 to 120 times as much being required as of cod-liver oil.

Continued overdoses of vitamin D, as in cod-liver oil, are dangerous, for it causes arterio-sclerosis and symptoms of premature senility. Babies have died from kidney trouble from being given too much cod-liver oil.

Persons using gland extracts without vitamin D get poor results.

There are comparatively few foods which contain enough D to be considered good sources, but ergosterol is changed into it by ultra-violet light. Hence foods containing D have it greatly enriched by irradiation with ultra-violet light.

The best sources of vitamin D are sun-baths, fish-liver oil, egg-yolks, butter and red salmon. Smaller amounts are found in milk, cream, liver, oysters and spinach.

Vitamin E. The Anti-sterility Vitamin

Vitamin E is essential to reproduction, and with vitamin B it is important during pregnancy and lactation.

Its absence causes abortions.

It is needed to prevent atrophy of the sex glands, but is not a sex stimulant. Its deficiency brings on frigidity, impotence, sterility, muscular debility, nervous impairment and inco-ordination.

In combination with A it is useful in eczema, hives and dermatitis. In anemic conditions it improves the skin color and tones up deflated tissues, although if taken in excess (such as too much spinach extract) it favors anemia.

In combination with F it is helpful in neuritic and arthritic pains, and enlarged prostate.

Combined with A it is helpful in dropsy, and combined with C it is useful in angina pectoris and cerebral hemorrhage.

It promotes the supply of calcium and magnesium to the tissues and prevents deposits of calcium around the joints and elsewhere.

Its deficiency causes loss of accommodation in both the lens and the iris of the eye.

It is not easily destroyed by heat.

Cancer in rats induced by the use of tar, has been reported by experimenters as cured by the use of vitamin E.

It occurs in small quantities in many foods, but most abundantly in the germ cells of cereals, especially wheat and corn, and in vegetable oils. Spinach, lettuce, watercress and fruits also contain fair amounts.

Vitamin F (Old B2). The Nutritional Vitamin

This is a fat-soluble vitamin indispensable to normal nutrition and healthy epithelial tissues.

It improves the circulation, and the skin color in anemia.

It co-operates with D in calcium control, but aggravates rickets if D is deficient.

Its deficiency tends to rough or peeling skin, giant hives, sores and ultimate eczema; brittle and falling hair, dandruff, brittle and ridged or fluted finger nails, frail bones in the aged, kidney irritation, hematuria, albuminuria, glycosuria and susceptibility to colds, distress in hot weather; also susceptibility to vitamin D poisoning, as it neutralizes the excess of D.

As a stimulant to the liver and bowels it is valuable in constipation. It is especially valuable in prostatic conditions.

"Vitamin F alone has so improved the accommodation of the eyes as to require a refitting of glasses, while in combination with A and C it makes the clearing up of cataracts much more rapid.

Stubborn cases of high blood pressure have yielded to its use.

It is worth a trial in all cases of feebleness in old age, as well as in arthritis and neuritis, for vitamin D loads the blood with calcium but F diffuses it to the tissues.

It is therefore indicated in kidney, bladder and gall stones.

It is also indicated in hay-fever, asthma and skin diseases.

Its most reliable sources are linseed oil, flaxseed, oatmeal, and especially rye. Small amounts are also found in milk and fish-liver oil.

Vitamin G (Old B1). The Pellagra and Cataract Vitamin

Vitamin G is essential to growth and well-being, and especially for the prevention of pellagra and cataract.

It is necessary to normal calcium absorption and red blood cell formation, and is therefore beneficial in anemia.

Age changes in the eyes are due to disordered calcium and vitamin functions. According to Hene there is a 500% increase in the calcium content of the eye lens between the ages of 34 and 56.

In test animals a deficiency of G almost invariably causes cataract (in 70 out of 72 rats tested), but in treating humans, G alone is not as useful as when combined with A, C and F. The time required for successful results with cataracts is from 4 to 14 months.

Combined with C vitamin G is helpful for vericose veins.

It is very soluble in water, but withstands considerable cooking, although it is destroyed by alkalies.

Its best source is the germ portion of cereals, green leaves, milk, eggs, yeast, cheese, and lean meats. Other fair sources are broccoli, cabbage, carrots, cauliflower, beets, peas, avacadoes, peanuts and soy beans.

SUMMARY

Vitamin A. Anti-infective

Essential to growth. Protects all mucous membranes. Protects against gall-stones.

Sources: Green and yellow leaves and vegetables, fruits, milk and its products, egg-yolks, liver, fish, oysters.

Vitamin B. Anti-neuritic

Protects nerves and brain.

Prevents Beriberi, goiter, rickets.

Necessary for absorption of starches and sweets, for peristalsis and endocrine functioning.

Very soluble in water.

Sources: Green and yellow vegetables, fruits, sweet potatoes, whole grains, nuts, milk, buttermilk, egg-yolks, fish, meats, organs.

Vitamin C. Anti-scurvy

Essential to growth, also to the teeth. Protects from pyorrhoea, rheumatism, weak bones, bruises, ulcers, high blood pressure, heart conditions.

Not stored. Easily killed.

Sources: Citrus fruits, greens, asparagus, cabbage, cauliflower, radishes, tomatoes, fruits, milk, organs.

Vitamin D. Anti-rickitic

Essential to growth of bones.

Protects from pneumonia, tuberculosis, ulcers, wrinkles, sunstroke.

Sources: Sunbaths, fish oils, butter, red salmon, milk, cream, liver, oysters, spinach.

Vitamin E. Anti-sterility

Protects from sterility, eczema, calcium deposits, loss of accommodation.

Sources: Cereal germs, vegetable oils, spinach, lettuce, watercress, fruits.

Vitamin F. Nutritional and Skin

Protects from skin disease, falling hair, brittle nails and bones, high blood pressure, hay-fever, asthma.

Sources: Linseed, flax seed, oatmeal, rye, milk, fish oils.

Vitamin G. Anti-Pellagra, Anti-cataract

Essential to growth, calcium absorption, cells.

Very soluble.

Sources: Cereals, greens, milk, cheese, eggs, meats, broccoli, cabbage, cauliflower, carrots, beets, peas, peanuts, soy beans.

TABLE OF FOODS ESPECIALLY RICH IN VITAMINS

The letter x indicates a fair amount, xx a good amount, and xxx the mimum amount of the vitamin indicated.

	Vitamins						
	A	B	C	D	E	F	G
Vegetables							
Artichokes	x	0	x	0	0	0	0
Asparagus	x	xxx	xxx	0	0	0	0
Beans, string	xxx	xx	xx	0	0	0	0
Beets	0	0	0	0	0	0	xx
Beet tops	xxx	xxx	xxx	0	0	0	xxx
Broccoli	xxx	xx	xx	0	0	0	xx
Brussels Sprouts	xx	0	xxx	0	0	0	0
Cabbage	xx	xxx	xxx	0	0	0	xx
Cantaloupes	xx	xx	xxx	0	0	0	0
Carrots	xxx	xxx	xx	0	0	0	xx
Cauliflower	x	xx	xxx	0	0	0	xx
Celery	0	xx	0	0	0	0	0
Chard	xxx	0	0	0	0	0	0
Collards	xxx	xxx	xxx	0	0	0	xx
Corn, green	x	xx	xx	0	xx	0	0
Cornmeal, yellow	x	xxx	0	0	0	0	0
Cucumbers	0	0	xx	0	0	0	0
Dandelions	xxx	0	0	0	0	0	0
Dock	xxx	0	0	0	0	0	0
Endive	x	0	xx	0	0	0	0
Flaxseed	x	xx	0	0	0	xxx	0
Grains,whole	0	xx	xx	0	0	0	xxx
Kale	xxx	xxx	0	0	0	0	xxx
Kohlrabbi	0	xx	xx	0	0	0	0
Leeks	0	xx	0	0	0	0	0
Lentils	0	xx	0	0	0	0	0
Lettuce	xxx	xx	xx	0	xx	0	0
Linseed	0	0	0	0	0	xxx	0
Oats	x	xx	0	0	0	xxx	0
Okra	xx	xx	0	0	0	0	0
Olives	xx	xx	xxx	0	xxx	0	xx
Onions	0	xx	xx	0	0	0	0
Parsley	xxx	0	xxx	0	0	0	0
Parsnips	xx	xxx	0	0	0	0	0
Peas, green	xxx	xxx	xxx	0	0	0	x
Peppers, green	xxx	xx	xxx	0	0	0	0

				Vitamins			
	A	B	C	D	E	F	G
Vegetables							
Potatoes, sweet	xxx	xx	xx	0	0	0	0
Potatoes, white	0	xx	xx	0	0	0	0
Pumpkin	x	x	x	0	0	0	0
Radishes	0	0	xxx	0	0	0	0
Rice, brown	0	xxx	0	0	0	0	0
Rutabagas	0	xx	xxx	0	0	0	0
Soy beans	0	0	0	0	0	0	xxx
Spinach	xxx	xxx	xxx	xxx	xxx	0	xxx
Squash, green	xxx	0	0	0	0	0	0
Squash, yellow	xxx	0	0	0	0	0	0
Tomatoes	xxx	xx	xxx	0	0	0	xx
Turnips	0	xx	xxx	0	0	0	0
Turnip tops	xxx	xxx	xxx	0	0	0	xxx
Vegetable oils	0	0	0	0	xxx	0	0
Wheat germs	0	0	0	0	xxx	0	xxx
Honey	0	xx	0	0	0	0	0
Proteins							
Beef, lean	0	xxx	0	0	0	0	xxx
Brains	0	xx	xxx	0	0	0	0
Butter	xxx	0	0	xx	0	0	0
Buttermilk	0	xx	0	0	0	0	xx
Cream	xx	x	0	xx	0	0	0
Cheese	xx	x	0	0	0	0	xxx
Chicken	0	xxx	0	0	0	0	xxx
Egg-yolks	xxx	xx	0	xxx	0	0	xx
Fish	0	xx	0	0	0	0	xx
Fish oils	xxx	0	0	xxx	0	xx	0
Fish roe	xxx	xx	0	0	0	0	0
Heart	0	xx	0	0	0	0	xxx
Kidney	xx	xx	xxx	0	0	0	xxx
Liver	xxx	xx	xx	xx	0	0	xxx
Milk	xx	xx	0	xx	0	xx	xxx
Oysters	xx	xx	0	xx	0	0	0
Salmon, red	xx	0	0	xx	0	0	xxx
Sardines	0	0	0	xx	0	0	0
Fruits							
Apricots	xxx						
Apples	0	0	xx	0	0	0	0

	Vitamins						
	A	B	C	D	E	F	G
Fruits							
Avocadoes	xx	xx	xx	0	0	0	xxx
Bananas	xx	xx	xx	0	0	0	xx
Berries	xx	0	xx	0	0	0	0
Cherries	xx	0	xx	0	0	0	0
Currants	0	0	xxx	0	0	0	0
Dates	xx	xx	0	0	0	0	0
Figs	0	xx	0	0	0	0	xx
Grapes	0	xx	0	0	0	0	0
Grapefruit	0	xx	xxx	0	0	0	xx
Guavas	0	0	xxx	0	0	0	0
Gooseberries	0	0	xx	0	0	0	0
Lemons	0	xx	xxx	0	0	0	0
Limes	0	0	xxx	0	0	0	0
Mangoes	xxx	0	xxx	0	0	0	0
Olives	0	xx	xxx	0	0	0	xx
Oranges	xx	xx	xxx	0	xxx	0	xx
Papaya	0	0	xx	0	0	0	0
Peaches	xxx	xx	xx	0	0	0	0
Pears	0	xx	0	0	0	0	xxx
Pineapples	0	xx	xx	0	0	0	0
Prunes	xxx	xx	0	0	0	0	0
Raspberries	0	0	xxx	0	0	0	0
Strawberries	0	0	xxx	0	0	0	0
Tangerines	0	0	xxx	0	0	0	0
Watermelons	0	xx	xx	0	xx	0	0
Nuts							
All contain moderate amounts of B, but peanuts add G.							

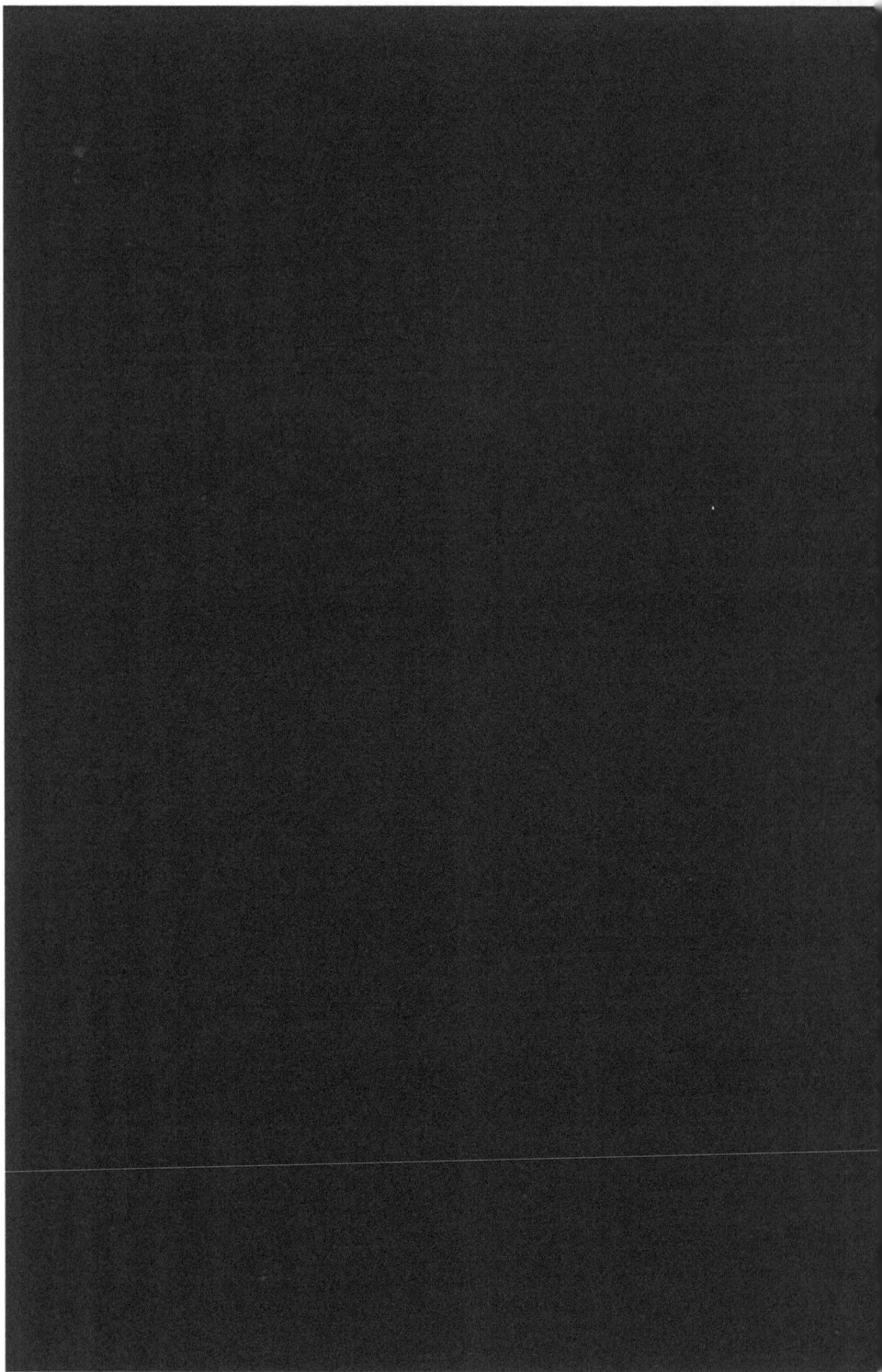

www.ingramcontent.com/pod-product-compliance
Lightning Source LLC
Chambersburg PA
CBHW071803020426
42331CB00008B/2384